RUNNING FOR OFFICE

A LOOK AT POLITICAL CAMPAIGNS

HOW GOVERNMENT WORKS

By Sandy Donovan

🔥 LERNER PUBLICATIONS COMPANY • MINNEAPOLIS

Lerner Publications Company
A division of Lerner Publishing Group
241 First Avenue North
Minneapolis, MN 55401 U.S.A.

Website address: www.lernerbooks.com

Library of Congress Cataloging-in-Publication Data

Donovan, Sandra, 1967–
    Running for office: a look at political campaigns / by Sandy Donovan.
        p.   cm. — (How government works)
    Summary: Describes what is involved in running a political campaign, from deciding to run for office through election night. Includes bibliographical references and index.
    ISBN: 0-8225-4700-7 (lib. bdg. : alk. paper)
    1. Political campaigns—United States—Juvenile literature. 2. Campaign management—United States—Juvenile literature. 3. Elections—United States—Juvenile literature. [1. Politics, Practical. 2. Elections.] I. Title. II. Series.
    JK2281.D66 2004
    324.7'0973—dc21   2003005613

Manufactured in the United States of America
1 2 3 4 5 6 – DP – 09 08 07 06 05 04

TABLE OF CONTENTS

INTRODUCTION:
ELECTIONS IN A DEMOCRACY

TRUE OR FALSE? The United States is a democracy. The answer is True. But do you know what it means to be a democracy? In a democracy, the government is run for the people and by the people. But citizens don't really do all the work. They choose other people called representatives to make decisions for them. These representatives help the government do its job.

People elect, or choose, their government representatives by voting. In the United States, we vote for

(Above) The U.S. Senate is one important group of elected representatives. Each state has two senators.

presidents, members of the U.S. Congress (the Senate and the House of Representatives), and governors. We also vote for school board members, judges, and many other elected officials. At school you might vote for student representatives, such as student body president and class treasurer.

Voting is an important right and a duty of all citizens in a democracy. When people use their right to vote, a democracy is strong.

Citizens in a democracy have another important right. We have the right to run for office. A person running for office is called a candidate. A candidate must officially file, or sign up, to run for a particular office. Then the candidate tries to get voters to vote for him or her. When many people run for office, voters have more choices. People vote for the candidate they think will best represent them and their ideas about the way the country should be governed.

So who should run for office? To be elected

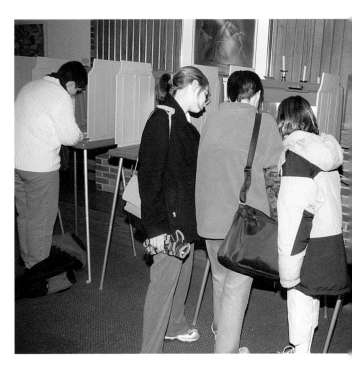

Young people watch their mother vote at her polling (voting) place.

to most government offices in the United States, candidates must be a certain age and a U.S. citizen. Running for office also requires a lot of hard work and dedication. It requires the ability to think quickly, to answer tough questions, and to accept criticism calmly.

The process is long and challenging. We're going to follow the steps taken by Samantha Brown (a fictional character) to run for the U.S. Senate. As we'll see, Brown discovers that running for office is hard but very rewarding. Elected officials get to help decide how to make a school, a town, a state, or even the whole country a better place to live.

Ralph Nader, a candidate for president in 2000, answers a reporter's questions.

CHAPTER 1
BROWN FOR SENATE

THINK ABOUT IT: What does it take to be a good candidate for political office? If you said the ability to think quickly and to answer tough questions, you are on the right track. But a candidate also needs time, money, experience, and the support of friends and family.

(Above) Former first lady Hillary Rodham Clinton announces that she will run for a U.S. Senate seat in New York in 2000.

Samantha Brown has been the popular mayor of Quillsville for six years. Her job has been to listen to the people of Quillsville and to help solve their problems. She helps the city

Rudolph Giuliani, the former mayor of New York City, discusses the mayor's job with students.

figure out how to best spend its money. She also proposes new laws to protect and help citizens. The city council, a group of elected officials who make decisions about the city, votes on these suggestions.

Brown likes being mayor. She feels she has made a difference in people's lives. Citizens told her that they were unhappy with the quality of the city's schools, so she helped get more money to hire more teachers. People complained about too much traffic in the city. Brown suggested spending more money on public buses. People started to ride the bus rather than drive their cars. Quillsville's traffic improved, and the roads needed fewer repairs.

The citizens of Quillsville have agreed with most of Mayor Brown's ideas to make the city better. Most people say she has done a good job. After her first term of four years, voters reelected her to a second term.

Brown says she is ready for a bigger challenge. She has helped improve her city, but she would like to help improve the rest of the state and the country. She wants to run for the U.S. Senate. She wants to be one of the two senators her state sends to Washington, D.C., where Congress meets. If elected, she can help make laws in Congress that will improve more people's lives.

WHAT IS CONGRESS?

Congress is a group of elected officials who write, debate, and make laws. It is made up of the House of Representatives and the Senate. The House includes representatives from each state. The number of representatives is based on how many people live in that state. Every state gets at least one representative, no matter how few people live there. All states have two senators. Each state is equally represented in the Senate regardless of its population.

The domed U.S. Capitol Building is a familiar landmark in Washington, D.C. It is also where Congress meets to make laws that affect the entire country.

A BIG COMMITMENT

Brown knows that running for office can be hard work, but she is used to working long hours. When she ran for mayor, she often slept only four hours a night. During the day, she campaigned. Campaigning includes all the work of running for office, such as meeting voters and giving speeches. To win elections, candidates want to make sure voters know who they are, what they think about the issues, and what they would do if elected.

But running for the U.S. Senate will be a tougher job than running for mayor. Brown will need to win votes across the whole state, not just in the town of Quillsville. Many people

SLOGANS

Most candidates pick one short saying that they repeat throughout an election. This saying is called a slogan. A candidate uses slogans to get people to remember what he or she stands for. When George H. W. Bush ran for president in 1988, his slogan was No New Taxes. Voters knew exactly what Bush believed in when they heard this slogan. What would your slogan be if you were running for president of your school?

I LIKE IKE

General Dwight Eisenhower, who served in World War II (1939–1945), had the nickname Ike. When Eisenhower ran for president in 1952, "I like Ike" was the slogan of his campaign.

This television ad says Rick Lazio's votes as a congressperson supported programs for senior citizens. With this ad, he hoped senior citizens would vote for him.

do not know who Brown is. Her opponents (the people she runs against) will try to make her look like a bad choice to the voters. Her opponents might say bad things about her job as mayor or about her views on certain issues. Brown and her family will have to be prepared for this.

Brown will have to spend a lot of money on her campaign. Running for senator is more expensive than running for mayor. Most voters get their information about a candidate from advertising. So Brown will have to spend money on television, radio, newspaper, and Internet

POLITICAL PARTIES

Political parties are groups of people who join together to gain control over the government. Members of a political party have similar beliefs about the way the government should be run. The United States has two main political parties: the Democratic Party and the Republican Party. In general, Democrats believe in a strong national government. Republicans believe in a smaller national government, with states having more power. Other political parties are usually called third parties. Third parties include the Libertarian Party and the Green Party. The Libertarian Party thinks the government should let citizens make most of their own decisions. The Green Party believes the government should work on such issues as keeping the environment clean and protecting workers' rights.

advertisements. These advertisements cost a lot of money.

Brown wants to see if this is a good time to run for senator. Senators serve six-year terms in Congress. But not all senators are elected in the same year. Next year, one of the current senators in Brown's state will be running for reelection. The other senator in Brown's state will be running for reelection two years later. Should Brown wait until then to run? Or does she have a good chance to win this time?

Brown has talked to many people about her decision to run for the U.S. Senate. She wants to make sure she is making the right decision. She talked to her husband and her two sons. She also talked to her closest friends. She talked to leaders of the political party she belongs to, the Democratic Party. She even talked to a former senator to find out what the job would be like.

Friends and family help Mazie Keiko Hirono *(far right)* campaign for governor of Hawaii.

It's Official

After all these discussions, Brown has decided to run next year. Her family told her that they would support her and work hard to help her win. They said they were prepared for her to work long hours. They also said they would ignore the bad things her opponents say about her.

Brown's friends also told her she should run. They said she has many good qualities for campaigning. She

Do This!

Read the newspaper or check out political party websites to find out about the candidates running for office in your town or state. What are these candidates saying about the issues and about their opponents?

At this gathering in 1988, Connecticut Democrat Joseph Lieberman *(at the podium)* announced he would run for the U.S. Senate. Lieberman won.

likes meeting new people. She is good at giving speeches. She can think quickly and answer difficult questions.

Democratic Party leaders told her that this is the right time for her to run for office. They like her ideas about how to improve the federal (national) government. They also said she has a good chance of beating the incumbent (current) senator, Charles Howe. Many voters are unhappy with his job so far.

Mayor Brown has made her decision, so it's time to get to work. She calls a press conference to announce that she is a candidate for the U.S. Senate. At press conferences, people answer questions from television and newspaper reporters.

Reporters from around the state come to hear Brown's announcement and to report what she has to say.

"If elected, I promise to work hard for the people," Brown says at her press conference. "Because of my work as mayor of Quillsville, I already know how to get things done in government."

Is Good Help Hard to Find?

Mayor Brown's press conference is in February. The election will be in November of the following year. Brown has almost two years of campaigning ahead of her.

Brown is prepared to work hard, but she knows she cannot win this election by herself. She will need an excellent staff to run her campaign. Her staff members will plan all her tasks and activities. They will raise the money

The new vice president Dick Cheney and his wife Lynne *(both standing)* thank campaign staff members for their work in George W. Bush's presidential campaign of 2000.

she needs for campaigning. They will produce her advertisements. They will help her answer difficult questions. They will oversee every piece of her campaign.

Having a good campaign staff is the key to a successful campaign. The first person Brown looks for is an experienced campaign manager. He or she will manage all the details of the campaign for the next two years.

Senator John F. Kennedy *(right)* ran for president in 1960. His brother Robert Kennedy *(left)* worked as John's campaign manager.

Brown knows just the person for the job—Ed Miguez. Miguez ran Brown's two successful campaigns for mayor, so he knows her well. He also managed winning campaigns for a U.S. congressman and for the governor of Brown's state. Miguez knows the concerns of the voters and the issues from around the state.

The next person Brown finds is a fund-raiser. This person will be in charge of raising enough money to pay for the campaign. Brown chooses Joe Washington. He is an expert at raising money for political campaigns. He knows which individuals and groups will support Brown's campaign.

In Concert at the Forum-April 15th · 8:30 PM

Carole King   Barbra Streisand   James Taylor

🎼¾ McGovern

Use the Power ⑱ Register and Vote

Quincy Jones and his Orchestra

Ushers: Warren Beatty · Jack Nicholson · Julie Christie · Sally Kellerman · James Earl Jones · Jacqueline Bisset
Michelle Gilliam · Mike Nichols · Shirley MacLaine · Goldie Hawn · Gene Hackman · Elliott Gould
Marlo Thomas · Burt Lancaster · Jon Voight · Raquel Welch · Michael Sarrazin · Britt Ekland and more

Celebrities gave a concert to raise money for George McGovern's 1972 campaign for president. Some even offered to be ushers.

Finally, Brown picks Alice Adams to be her treasurer. The treasurer keeps track of campaign money and pays all the bills. This is a difficult job because there are many rules about how campaigns can raise and spend money. These rules are called campaign finance laws. The treasurer has to know all these laws because he or she has to file the necessary financial reports during the campaign.

CHAPTER 2
FIRST UP:
THE PRIMARY ELECTION

QUICK QUESTION: Samantha Brown has her campaign staff. But what is the next step? If you answered campaigning, you are correct. So how does Brown begin campaigning?

Republican presidential candidate Senator Phil Gramm *(center)* listens carefully to a young supporter while campaigning in Iowa.

Brown's campaign manager knows how to campaign. Miguez knows that the goal of the campaign is to get Brown elected to the Senate.

From that goal, Miguez works backward to plan the campaign.

Each state has its own rules for selecting candidates for the general election. Brown's state uses primary elections. In a primary election, people vote for which candidates will run in the general election.

In Brown's state, the primary election takes place in June, five months before the general election. To win the primary, Brown has to receive more votes than any of the other Democratic candidates running for Senate. So Brown's campaign needs to convince people to vote for her in June.

Did You KNOW? Each state that holds a primary election has its own rules and schedule for running a primary.

GETTING KNOWN

The citizens of Quillsville already know Brown and will probably vote for her in the primary. In the rest of the state, however, voters do not know much about Brown. Her campaign manager has to introduce Brown to voters around the state. Then Brown has to convince them to support her.

Brown travels around the state to meet voters. She goes from town to town. She visits cities and farming communities. She has coffee at local cafes and talks to voters. She tells them why she wants to be their senator. She asks them what they think about different state and national issues. She talks about education, jobs, and the environment. She tells voters what she wants to do in Congress. She is trying to convince them to vote for her in the primary election.

CONVENTIONS

Many voters try to find out what each candidate has to say. They want to make a good decision about whom to vote for in the primary.

But other voters do not have time to learn about every candidate on the primary election ballot. They want political parties to recommend, or endorse, the best candidate. Each political party usually endorses one candidate out of the many people running for the party's nomination. Generally, this is the candidate whose ideas the party leaders most agree with and who has the best chance of winning the general election.

Do This! How do candidates get their names on the primary election ballot in your state? Check out the secretary of state website for your state to find out what the rules are.

Democrat David Bonior has represented Michigan in the U.S. House of Representatives since 1976. An incumbent such as Bonior usually gets his or her party's endorsement at election time.

Arizona senator John McCain addresses the California Republican Party convention. He hoped to win his party's endorsement to run for president in 2000.

Getting her party's endorsement would really help Brown win the primary election. So Brown and her staff try to win the endorsement. Brown attends local party meetings. She and her staff members talk to party leaders around the state.

The Democrats in Brown's state hold a large meeting called a state convention. The convention is held at the Quillsville Convention Center in March—three months before the primary election. Candidates, delegates, important party members, and news reporters fill the convention center. Brown gives a fifteen-minute speech. She talks about the issues that are important to voters in the state.

CAUCUSES AND CONVENTIONS

In some states, political parties nominate and endorse candidates for the general election at caucuses. Caucuses are meetings of people interested in a party's goals. Each political party may hold small caucuses at schools or community centers around the state. At these meetings, people discuss issues and candidates. They also vote for delegates at caucuses. Delegates represent their caucus at larger district, state, and national meetings called conventions. Each political party holds a statewide convention as well as a national convention.

"The high cost of health care is a major concern for voters," she says. "In the last year, I have traveled all over the state. I have listened to voters. If you endorse me as the Democratic candidate for Senate, I will win this election. I will go to Washington and fight for more affordable health care."

Finally, the delegates take a vote to endorse a candidate for the senate race. Four candidates are trying to win the endorsement. Brown knows she has a lot of support, so she feels confident. All of the delegates vote, and Brown receives 60 percent of their votes! The other

Supporters congratulate Senator Paul Wellstone in 1996. He had won the Minnesota Democratic-Farmer-Labor Party (Democratic Party) convention's endorsement to run for reelection.

candidates only receive about 10 percent each.

Brown has won her party's endorsement. She gives a brief acceptance speech. She tells party members that she will do her best to represent Democrats in the state.

"I know we will win this election next November," she tells them.

FIRST VOTE: PRIMARY ELECTION DAY

Winning the party's endorsement is only the first step in a long campaign for Brown. In a couple of months, statewide voters will choose an official Democratic candidate in the primary election. Many Democratic voters will vote for Brown because she has the party's endorsement. But some voters will vote for the other candidates. Brown wants to win these people's votes too. She continues to give speeches and to meet voters. She also creates a website and produces television and radio ads to reach more voters.

GETTING ON THE BALLOT

Sometimes candidates who do not win an endorsement run in the election anyway. These candidates have a hard time winning because they do not have the support of a political party. They can get on the ballot by filing a petition. A petition is a statement signed by many people with a specific goal, such as getting a candidate's name on the primary ballot. It takes hundreds or even thousands of signatures to get on the ballot. Contacting that many people is a big task. Volunteers begin by talking to supporters. Then volunteers go door-to-door and get more people to sign the petition. They also go to shopping malls and large events to get voters' signatures.

On primary election day, polling places open at 7:00 A.M. Brown gets up early and is first in line to vote at her polling place. She votes for herself and then spends the rest of the day on a get-out-the-vote campaign. At 8:00 P.M., the polling places close. There is nothing to do but wait for the results. Computers count most of the ballots, so it does not take long. At 10:00 P.M., the ballots are all counted. Brown has won the primary election!

OPEN AND CLOSED PRIMARIES

In many states, when citizens register to vote, they have to choose, or register for, a political party. Then, in primary elections, voters can only vote for the candidates from that party. These are called closed primaries. Other states hold open primaries. At the time of the open primary, voters can choose which party's candidates they will be voting for. Voters do not have to be registered for a particular party to vote for that party's candidate.

Brown walks into the ballroom of the Quillsville Grand Hotel. Cameras flash. Hundreds of party members fill the room. They applaud as Brown takes the microphone. Her campaign staff has spent many days writing a victory speech for this night.

"This is just the beginning of our victory," Brown tells the crowd. She is already thinking ahead to the general election in November.

CHAPTER 3
CAMPAIGNING:
THE RACE FOR THE SENATE

QUICK QUESTION: Brown has won the party's endorsement for the U.S. Senate race. Can she relax until the general election?

Absolutely not! The hard work of campaigning is just beginning. On Election Day in November, Brown will face two opponents for the Senate seat. One is Senator Charles Howe, who is running

Incumbent senator Carol Mosely Braun of Illinois hopes for the best in the close 1998 race for her Senate seat.

for reelection. He is a Republican. The other candidate is a Green Party member named Ryan Hu.

THE ISSUES

For the next five months, the three candidates will discuss many issues that affect people throughout the state. Each candidate will try to convince voters that his or her positions, or beliefs, on these issues are best for the state and for the country. Brown tells voters what her positions are on health care, jobs, and the environment.

Brown thinks the government should make sure everyone has health care. Brown also says she will vote to raise the minimum wage to seven dollars an hour. The minimum wage is the lowest amount of money businesses can pay workers for their labor.

Among the most famous debates in U.S. history were the Lincoln-Douglas debates in their 1858 U.S. Senate race. Abraham Lincoln (*at the podium*) and Stephen A. Douglas (*behind Lincoln*) toured Illinois to argue over issues such as slavery.

DEBATES

Debates have been a popular campaign activity for hundreds of years. In a political debate, candidates discuss their opinions about issues important to voters. Preparing for debates takes a lot of time. Candidates have to be prepared to answer any question that may be asked. Have you ever participated in a debate or seen one on television?

President George H. W. Bush talks to students about environmental issues in 1990. They are in a National Park Service environmental education program at the Everglades National Park in Florida.

"Food, clothing, and housing cost more every year, and workers are not earning enough money to support their families," she says. Finally, Brown says that she will help make the air and water cleaner by passing strict laws about polluting.

Senator Howe says that Brown's ideas will cost too much money. This money comes from taxes the government collects from citizens.

"The citizens of this state already pay too much in taxes," Howe says. "Businesses should pay for their workers' health care. And we do not need to spend government money on the environment. Citizens and businesses can take care of the environment without the government's help."

The Green Party candidate Ryan Hu agrees with many of Brown's positions. He agrees that the government should provide health care for everyone. He also agrees that the minimum wage should be raised. But Hu's strongest position concerns the environment.

"Companies should not be allowed to dump waste into rivers and lakes," Hu says. "I will vote for laws that stop this activity."

ON THE CAMPAIGN TRAIL

Howe has been a senator for more than five years, so many voters already know him. It is hard to win a race against an incumbent. Brown knows she cannot waste any time. Her campaign has to tell voters why she should be the next senator. To do this, her staff members plan many campaign activities. Her staff runs television and radio ads. The ads talk about Brown's success as Quillsville's mayor. They also explain how Brown will be a better senator than Howe has been.

Brown's staff members also plan and design campaign literature. Campaign literature is written material, usually small flyers, that talks about a candidate's background and

Adlai Stevenson used a lot of campaign literature in his campaign for president in 1952.

Staff members recruit volunteers at the Robert F. Kennedy for President headquarters in Washington, D.C., in 1968.

positions on the issues. Brown's volunteers hand out these flyers throughout the state. The volunteers go door-to-door and talk to voters about Brown.

Brown's staff members write statements called press releases, or news releases, to send to major state newspapers every day. These statements talk about Brown's positions on the issues. Not all the news releases get printed, but when they do, more people will see Brown's name in

VOLUNTEERS

Volunteers are an important part of every campaign. Campaigns hire staff to do much of the work. But a candidate usually can't afford to pay enough people to do all the work. This is why volunteers are so important. Volunteers often perform tasks such as stuffing campaign literature into envelopes. Volunteers also walk door-to-door throughout neighborhoods and talk to voters about their candidate. Sometimes volunteers put up large yard signs with the candidate's name on them. On Election Day, volunteers even drive voters who need rides to the polling places so they can vote. Even if you're not old enough to drive, you can help hand out literature or stuff envelopes for a campaign.

PACS: POLITICAL ACTION COMMITTEES

A political action committee, or PAC, is a group of people who combine their resources to support one issue or candidate in an election. A PAC can represent a business interest, such as insurance companies or health care workers. A PAC can also represent people with similar views, such as those opposed to citizens owning handguns. PACs have great influence in elections because they are allowed to donate more money to candidates than individuals are. The law says an individual person can only donate $2,000 to a candidate in each election. A PAC can donate up to $5,000 to one candidate's campaign. And members of a PAC can each give their $2,000 contribution to the PAC. PACs can also spend additional money on advertisements to support a candidate.

print. Some of these people will decide to vote for her.

Brown's days are full from morning to night. Every morning she gets up early and meets with her campaign staff. They tell her voters' concerns. They also tell her what her opponents are saying and doing in their campaigns.

As mayor of Quillsville, Brown has city business to take care of during the day. She wants to make sure she is still doing a good job as mayor.

Members of the United Auto Workers union (UAW) *(above)* supported candidates who would vote for laws their PAC favors.

In the evenings, Brown campaigns. She continues to travel around the state and meet voters. She also gives several speeches a week.

Brown is busy sixteen hours a day, seven days a week. She has to meet as many voters as she can before November.

"SOUND BYTE" " Hey, I won the election. I don't have to kiss babies anymore."
—Clint Eastwood, actor and new mayor of Carmel-by-the-Sea, California, in 1987

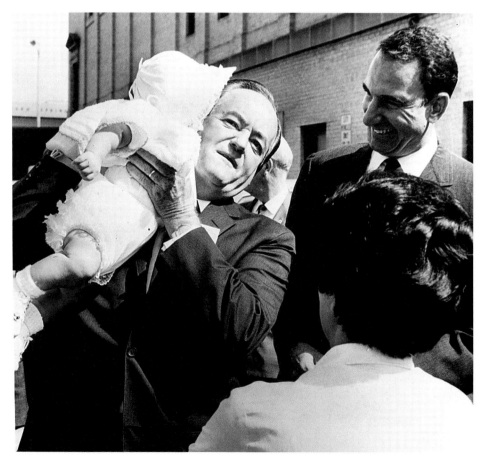

Vice President Hubert Humphrey holds a baby during the presidential campaign of 1968. He hopes the child's parents will vote for him.

In 1986 President Ronald Reagan *(left)* supported Linda Chavez *(right)* for the U.S. Senate. He appeared on stage with Chavez at a fund-raiser for her.

RAISING MONEY TO PAY THE BILLS

Campaigning costs money. Advertising is expensive. Printing campaign literature is expensive. Traveling around the state is expensive. Fund-raising, or raising money, is an important task of any campaign. Brown's fund-raiser is in charge of finding ways to raise money for her campaign.

Fund-raising events are a great way to collect money quickly. Brown's campaign raises a lot of money by holding fancy dinners for wealthy Democrats. At one fund-raiser, they raise more than

Did You KNOW? In 2002 the average money spent on a U.S. Senate campaign was $3.2 million!

$1 million dollars in one night. The president of the United States, who supports Brown, comes to Quillsville for the fund-raiser. More than one thousand guests attend. They pay $1,000 each to come to the dinner.

Brown's campaign also gets many smaller donations from other Democrats. Staff members call people and send letters asking for donations. But campaign finance laws set limits for how much money each person or business can give to a campaign. Some wealthy Democrats give the maximum amount of $2,000 each. More often, people send checks for $100, $50, or $25.

TURNING POINT In 1971 the Federal Election Campaign Act (FECA) became the major law that limits campaign spending.

CHAPTER 4
ELECTION DAY: THE FINISH LINE

QUICK QUESTION: Does a candidate get nervous in the last few days before an election? Maybe. But he or she probably doesn't have time to be nervous at all.

In the days before the election, Brown is busier than ever. One day she appears on a call-in radio show. Listeners call the station and ask her questions about the issues.

The secret ballot (*above*) wasn't used in the United States until 1889. Before that, U.S. voters had to say out loud or show with hands how they were voting.

"I can't get a job because I can't afford to pay for day care while I work," says one caller. "What will you do for people like me?"

"I'm glad you asked that," Brown replies. "There are many people like you all over the state, and we need to help them. As a senator, I will look for ways to make child care more affordable. I also think the minimum wage should be raised to help pay for things like child care."

Another caller asks Brown what her husband and children will do if she wins the election. Brown says that her family will stay in Quillsville, and she will come home from Washington every weekend. This will also help her stay in touch with the concerns of the people in her state.

New York City mayor, Rudolph Giuliani (left), discusses issues with listeners on a call-in radio show in 1995.

How Am I Doing?

Political campaigns spend a lot of time trying to figure out how their candidate is going to do in an election. To do this, they use polling. Polling is a system of questioning voters about whom they plan to vote for. A few hundred people from one area get telephone calls asking which candidates they will support and what issues are important to them. Based on what those few hundred people said, the pollsters predict how the rest of the voters will vote. Polls also ask people questions about their age, their income, and even their religion. Campaigns use this information to try to figure out what types of people will vote for which candidates. For instance, wealthy people often vote for one type of candidate, and single parents often vote for another.

Have you ever been asked to participate in a poll? Try polling students at your school to find out how they feel about an issue.

(Left to right) Warren Mitofski from the CBS-*New York Times* poll, Dr. George Gallup from Gallup Polls, and Louis Harris from Harris Polls discuss the results of the 1980 presidential race.

Former senator and vice president Walter Mondale *(center top)* came out of retirement to run for Senator Paul Wellstone's seat in 2002. Mondale's campaign was brief. Wellstone died in a plane crash less than one month before the election.

In addition to radio shows, Brown attends big meetings called rallies. These rallies take place in shopping centers, schools, town halls, and other locations around the state. Voters go to rallies to show their support for a candidate. Brown goes to rallies for Democratic candidates running for other offices, such as governor or the state legislature. (The state legislature is the lawmaking body of government in the state that does the same job as Congress does for the country.) Each Democratic candidate at these rallies gives a short speech, and the crowd cheers.

ELECTION DAY

After a blur of speeches and rallies, Election Day finally arrives. Election Day is Brown's last chance to convince people to vote for her. She wakes up early and meets with

WHO CAN VOTE?

All U.S. citizens over the age of eighteen are allowed to vote in elections. To vote in most states, people must first register their names and addresses with the state. Election judges check the list of registered voters to make sure voters don't vote more than once in the same election. But sometimes registration limits voting because people do not know how or where to register. In 1995 Congress passed the Voter Registration Act. This law made it easier for people to register to vote. It says that states must allow people to register to vote at their polling place or when they apply for or renew a driver's license.

A voter *(left)* checks in at her polling place in Dearborn, Michigan.

her campaign manager. They discuss their plans for the day.

At 7:00 A.M., Brown goes to her polling place. News cameras film her walking in to cast her vote. When she comes out, she smiles at the camera and makes a victory sign with her hand.

From the polling place, Brown goes to a rally outside Quillsville City Hall. Hundreds of supporters show up to cheer for her. Many have large signs reading "Brown for Senate." After the rally, she tries to talk to as many people as possible. She walks down busy streets and asks people to support her. Many people are happy to see her and want to shake her hand. They wish her luck in the election.

Did You KNOW? Election Day is always the first Tuesday after the first Monday in November.

Meanwhile, Brown's campaign staff is hard at work. Staff members will try to get as many Brown supporters to the polling places as they can.

Many of Brown's supporters are poor. Some do not own cars and do not have the time to take a bus to their polling place. Others have small children whom they cannot leave alone while they vote. Volunteers from Brown's campaign offer to drive many people to their polling place. They also offer to baby-sit children while parents vote. One thing volunteers cannot do, however, is to pay someone to vote. That's illegal in America.

In every state, thousands of volunteers, such as this woman, call voters to remind them to vote on Election Day.

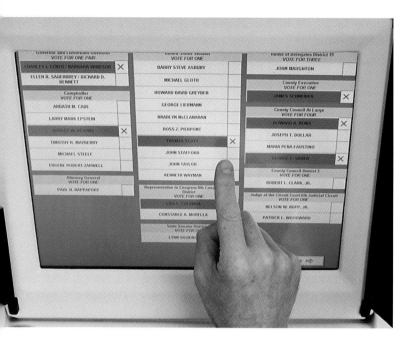

In some modern elections, voters might use a computer screen *(above)* to choose candidates for office.

ELECTION NIGHT

Brown spends the day appearing at rallies, giving speeches, and meeting voters. At 8:00 P.M., the polling places close. Brown waits for the results. This is the hardest part of the campaign for her. She is used to being busy every minute.

Brown and her family are in a hotel room at the Quillsville Grand Hotel. This hotel is the state's Democratic headquarters for the night. Democratic candidates for each race in the state also wait to hear election results. Downstairs, the Grand Ballroom is decorated for victory parties. Red, white, and blue streamers hang from every corner.

DIG DEEPER In most U.S. national elections, only about 50 percent of qualified voters actually vote. Why do you think that is?

LEARN THE LINGO

A precinct is a voting district in a city or town. Each precinct has its own polling place.

Party leaders, volunteers, activists, and television reporters wait for news.

Upstairs, Brown is on the phone to her campaign manager. Staff members have been tracking election results as they come in.

Slowly, precincts (voting areas) across the state report their results. At 8:00 P.M., only a few of the precincts have reported their votes. Senator Howe is winning with 65 percent of those votes. Brown has 28 percent, and the Green Party candidate has only 7 percent. Since so few votes have

Television networks once used big boards to show election results. Computers usually do this work in modern elections.

George W. Bush *(second from left)* had to wait for weeks for the results of the 2000 presidential election that sent him to the White House.

come in, Brown is not discouraged. Her campaign manager told her that these precincts would probably vote for Howe.

By 10:00 P.M., half of the precincts have reported their votes. Howe and Brown are tied. Each has 46 percent of the vote. Soon Brown begins to take a lead. She watches as more of the precincts' votes are counted. She is leading with 55 percent of the vote. By the time most of the votes are counted, the television reporters are announcing that Brown will be the winner. Computers are used to determine what the final results will be.

Brown hugs her family, but it is not time to announce her victory yet. Many of her friends and staff members call her hotel room to congratulate her. She tells them it is not over yet, but she knows that she has won.

At 10:30 P.M., an important phone call comes. It is Senator Howe. He is calling to congratulate her. He says she has run a good campaign. He wishes her luck in Washington. He says he will concede (admit defeat) in the next few minutes. This means he will publicly announce that he has lost the race. Although 15 percent of the vote has not been counted yet, he knows he has lost.

Rick Lazio concedes (admits defeat) to Hillary Rodham Clinton in 2000. Clinton became the new U.S. senator from New York.

(Left to right) Vice President-elect Al Gore, Tipper Gore, Hillary Clinton, and President-elect Bill Clinton celebrate their victory in the 1992 presidential election.

VICTORY PARTY

At 10:45 P.M., Brown and her family enter the Grand Ballroom. They smile and raise their hands to the crowd. The crowd cheers wildly as balloons fill the room. Brown walks to the microphone and begins her victory speech. She wrote the speech almost six months ago, in anticipation of this moment.

LEARN THE LINGO

The newly elected president is called the president-elect. A candidate for Senate is called the senator-elect after she or he is elected.

"We did it!" Brown begins as the crowd cheers. "We are going to Washington, and we are going to make a difference," she says. She thanks her family and her staff for all their hard work. She says she could not have won without the help of all of them.

WHAT HAPPENS NEXT?

After almost two years of campaigning, Samantha Brown has won the U.S. Senate election. On election night, she will celebrate her victory with other Democratic Party members and with her family. And tomorrow she can sleep in for the first time in months. She's worn out after all that campaigning.

But Brown still has a lot of work to do before becoming a senator. She needs to hire a staff to help her prepare for her job.

In January Brown will go to Washington, D.C. She will begin her term as Senator Brown. She will have offices in Washington and in Quillsville. In her first few months, she will learn a lot about what a senator does.

Dianne Feinstein is sworn in as a senator from California in 1992. She officially becomes a senator by taking the oath of office.

In the near future, Brown will think about running for re-election in six years. She already knows firsthand that campaigning is a lot of work. She will have to decide if she will do it all over again.

KIDS COUNT!

Maybe you can't vote yet, but you can still be a part of the election and voting processes. Read on to find out how kids just like you get involved.

CHECK IT OUT

To find out more about how government works in your area, you'll have to do some detective work. In modern campaigns, learning more about the candidates and issues is as easy as clicking a mouse. Most political parties and candidates have websites with loads of information about who they are and what they do. Many websites even have a section for kids, so you can find out how to be part of a political campaign.

You can also read the newspaper or watch the news on television to find out about elections. Stations such as C-SPAN cover politics twenty-four hours a day. You can see the U.S. Congress and even the British Parliament in action.

WRITE A LETTER

What you think matters. Write letters to local, state, or national officials. Tell them what you know about them and their views on certain issues. Ask candidates how they feel about other issues that concern you. (See p. 53 for instructions for writing to your U.S. senators and representatives.)

SCHOOL ELECTIONS

Be a student representative. Most schools have a student council or government. Find out how to be a part of it. Become a member or help a friend run for office. Poll your classmates. Ask what changes the students would like to see at school. What do they want? What don't they want? Make sure you ask people with many different interests and hobbies. You want your student government to represent all the students in your school, not just a few! Advertise—make posters saying what you would do for the school if you were elected. Use campaign slogans to say what you'll do in office, such as "For a student council that's really great, use your brain and vote for Kate!"

VOLUNTEER

Some campaign activities can be done by anyone. You can pass out campaign literature or help staff members set up activities. Contact a candidate for office and find out what kids can do to help out the campaign.

MOCK ELECTIONS

Create your own general election at school for kids to vote in. You and your classmates can vote for whom you think should be the next mayor, governor, congressperson, senator, or even president. Research the candidates, make campaign posters, set up polling places, and count the votes. See how the results at your school match those of the real general election.

GET OUT THE VOTE

Kids can help get out the vote for local, state, and national elections. Remind parents, teachers, and other adults to register to vote. Tell them how much their vote counts, especially since you can't vote yet. Ask them if you can come to the registration place with them. Some states even have booths for kids to cast their votes alongside registered voters on Election Day. Your vote won't officially count, but you'll learn how voting works. And when you're eighteen years old, you can make your vote count.

THE CLOSE UP PROGRAM

Perhaps the best way to find out more about how government works is to see it up close. That's the purpose of the Close Up program. Every year more than 25,000 people travel to Washington, D.C., to learn the ins and outs of the U.S. government. Students spend the week interacting with elected officials and visiting national and historical monuments. Students in grades six through eight learn about U.S. history and conflicts. High-school students participate in discussions about all aspects of government—from defense to international relations. Close Up also has programs for students interested in learning about city or state governments. Check out the website <www.closeup.org> for information on all Close Up programs.

RUNNING FOR OFFICE AT A GLANCE

DECIDE TO RUN
> Do your research—Talk to people about running for office. Find out what the job is like and if you are qualified to do it.
> Announce your candidacy.
> File the necessary forms.

GET ORGANIZED
> Hire a staff.
> Recruit volunteers.

MAKE A PLAN
> Determine a schedule—Decide what needs to be done and who will do it.
> Estimate how much money you'll need, and figure out how you'll get it.

CAMPAIGN
> Win support—Talk to voters about who you are, what issues are important to you, and what you plan to do in office.
> Advertise—Print and pass out campaign literature. Design a website. Produce television, newspaper, and radio advertisements.
> Give speeches.
> Poll your voters.

GET ON THE BALLOT
> Attend caucuses and conventions.
> Get the support of your political party, or collect signatures on a petition.
> Vote in the primary election. Wait for the results. Winners continue to campaign for the general election. Losers start to plan for the next time they can run.

THE GENERAL ELECTION
> Vote.
> Get out the vote—Do last-minute campaigning.
> Wait for the results.

CELEBRATE OR START OVER
> Winners take office. Losers prepare for the next election.

GLOSSARY

ballot: the document on which a voter marks his or her choice in an election. A ballot can be a piece of paper, a punch card, or a voting machine.

campaign: the work of trying to help a candidate win an election. Campaigning includes work by the candidate and many other people.

campaign finance laws: various state and federal (national) laws that limit how campaigns can raise and spend money

campaign manager: the person on a campaign staff who runs the campaign. He or she manages all the details of a campaign.

caucus: a meeting of political party members from individual precincts (voting areas) to discuss issues, endorse candidates, and vote for delegates

congressperson: a member of the U.S. House of Representatives; also called a congressman or congresswoman

convention: a large state or national meeting of delegates in a political party. This kind of meeting is used to determine a party's position on issues and to choose candidates for office.

delegates: people who will represent party members at district, state, and national meetings

Election Day: the national day set aside for voting to select the winner of presidential and congressional races. It's the first Tuesday after the first Monday in November.

endorse: the decision by a political party to support one candidate, usually from among the many people running for a particular position

fund-raiser: the member of a campaign staff who is in charge of raising money for a campaign; also, an event to raise money for a campaign

general election: the final election in which voters select the candidates for office

petition: a written request, usually signed by many people. Candidates without party support often have to send in petitions in order to run in primary elections. The petition shows that many voters support the candidate.

political party: a group of people who join together to gain political power. Also called a party. People who belong to a political party often have similar beliefs about the way the government should be run.

polling: a system of questioning voters about whom they plan to vote for. Polling is usually done over the telephone.

polling place: the official place where residents vote in their neighborhood. Polling places may be in churches, government buildings, or schools.

press conference: a meeting of news reporters to interview an important person, such as a politician, who is making an announcement

press release: written statements sent to the media that describe a candidate's activities or positions; also called a news release

primary election: an election in which voters choose which candidates will run in the general election

register: to enroll oneself as a voter by providing one's name and address, proof of citizenship, eligibility to vote, etc.

representative: a person who acts on behalf of a group of people. Members of the U.S. or states' House of Representatives are also called representatives.

staff: a group of people who do paid work for an organization. A campaign staff usually includes a campaign manager, a finance chairperson, a treasurer, and many other workers.

state legislature: a group of elected officials who has the power to make laws for a state

term: the set number of years that an elected official stays in office once he or she is elected. A U.S. senator's term is six years. The U.S. president's term is four years.

treasurer: the member of a staff who keeps track of money and pays all the bills for a campaign or organization

SOURCE NOTES

For quoted material: p. 31, "No More Baby Kissing," *TIME.com: TIME Magazine Archive,* April 6, 1987, <http://www.time.com/time/archive/preview/from_search/0,10987,1101870406-146309,00.html> (July 25, 2003).

BIBLIOGRAPHY

Bike, William S. *Winning Political Campaigns: A Comprehensive Guide to Electoral Success.* Juneau, AK: Denali Press, 1998.

Herrnson, Paul S. *Congressional Elections: Campaigning at Home and in Washington.* Washington, D.C.: Congressional Quarterly Press, 2000.

Jantzen, Steven. *Scholastic American Citizenship.* New York: Scholastic Book Services, 1980.

Simpson, Dick. *Winning Elections.* New York: HarperCollins, 1996.

FURTHER READING AND WEBSITES

BOOKS

Bonner, Mike. *How to Become an Elected Official.* New York: Chelsea House Publishers, 2000.

De Capua, Sarah. *Running for Public Office.* New York: Children's Press, 2002.

Donovan, Sandy. *Making Laws: A Look at How a Bill Becomes a Law.* Minneapolis: Lerner Publications Company, 2004.

Feldman, Ruth Tenzer. *How Congress Works: A Look at the Legislative Branch.* Minneapolis: Lerner Publications Company, 2004.

Heath, David. *Elections in the United States.* Mankato, MN: Bridgestone Books, 1999.

Kowalski, Kathiann. *A Balancing Act: A Look at Checks and Balances.* Minneapolis: Lerner Publications Company, 2004.

Kronenwetter, Michael. *Political Parties of the United States.* Berkeley Heights, NJ: Enslow Publishers, 1996.

Landau, Elaine. *Friendly Foes: A Look at Political Parties.* Minneapolis: Lerner Publications Company, 2004.

Majure, Janet. *Elections.* San Diego: Lucent Books, 1996.

WEBSITES

Ben's Guide to U.S. Government for Kids
<http://bensguide.gpo.gov/6-8/election/index.html> (for grades six to eight)
<http://bensguide.gpo.gov/3-5/election/index.html> (for grades three to five)
This guide to the U.S. government has details about the election process.

Democratic National Committee
430 South Capitol Street SE
Washington, D.C. 20003-4024
<http://www.democrats.org>
Contact this group or check out its website to get information on Democratic candidates or party positions on issues around the country.

The Gallup Organization (Gallup Poll)
<http://www.gallup.com/>
Read briefings on the results of recent opinion polls, news releases, journal articles, and more.

Green Party of the United States
PO Box 57065
Washington, DC 20037
<http://www.gp.org>
This website provides information on Green Party positions and candidates.

Harris Interactive (Harris Poll®)
<http://www.harrisinteractive.com/>
Read articles summarizing the topics and results of past opinion polls.

Kids Voting USA
<http://www.kidsvotingusa.org>
This website features information on how kids can get involved in the election process around the country.

Kid's World Government Page
<http://now2000.com/kids/government.shtml>
This page has lots of information and links to help you find out more about the government and politics of the United States.

League of Women Voters of the United States
1730 M Street NW
Washington, D.C. 20036
<http://www.lwv.org>
This organization's goal is to educate the public about elections. Look in the phone book to find a local chapter, or write to the national office above if you have questions about elections in your state. The League's website has links to information about candidates in all fifty states.

Libertarian Party
2600 Virginia Ave. NW
Suite 100
Washington, D.C. 20037
<http://www.lp.org/>
This website provides information on Libertarian Party positions and candidates.

Project Vote Smart
129 NW Fourth Street, Suite 204
Corvalis, OR 97330
<http://www.vote-smart.org>
Contact this national organization to get information about candidates for state and federal offices around the United States. Project Vote Smart's website has lots of information for voters, particularly about presidential candidates. Check out their Youth Inclusion Project for tips on how kids can become involved in elections.

Republican National Committee
310 First Street SE
Washington, D.C. 20003-1801
<http://www.gop.com>
Contact this group or check out its website to get information on Republican candidates or party positions on issues around the country.

TO WRITE YOUR U.S. SENATOR OR REPRESENTATIVE

You can write to your U.S. Senator or Representative. The address for a senator is

The Honorable [senator's full name]
United States Senate
Washington, D.C. 20510

The address for a representative is

The Honorable [representative's full name]
United States House of Representatives
Washington, D.C. 20515

Start your letter to a senator with, "Dear Senator [senator's last name]. Start your letter to a representative with, "Dear Mr. or Ms. (or Representative, Congressman, or Congresswoman) [representative's last name]. Tell them clearly who you are, what school you go to, and what you'd like to say. Include your address.

INDEX

ABOUT THE AUTHOR

Sandy Donovan has written many books for young readers, on topics including history, civics, and biology. She has also worked as a newspaper reporter and a political magazine editor. She holds a bachelor's degree in journalism and political science and a master's degree in public policy. She lives in Minneapolis with her husband and two sons. Donovan's other titles include *Making Laws: A Look at How a Bill Becomes a Law, Protecting America: A Look at the People Who Keep Our Country Safe,* and *The Channel Tunnel.*

PHOTO ACKNOWLEDGMENTS

Photographs in this book appear with the permission of: © United States Senate Photo Studio, p. 4; © Todd Strand/Independent Picture Service, pp. 5, 37; © Jim West, pp. 6, 20, 38, 39; © AFP/CORBIS, pp. 7, 15, 25; © Richard B. Levine, pp. 8, 43; © A.A.M. Van der Heyden Collection/Independent Picture Service, p. 9; © Bettmann/CORBIS, pp. 10, 14, 16, 32, 36, 41; © Frances M. Roberts, pp. 11, 35; © Photo by Paul J. Buklarewicz, p. 13; © David J. & Janice L. Frent Collection/CORBIS, p. 17; © Robert Maass/CORBIS, p. 18; © Reuters NewMedia Inc./CORBIS, pp. 21, 42; AP/Wide World Photos, pp. 22, 29; © Independent Picture Service, p. 26; George Bush Presidential Library, p. 27; © Wally McNamee/ CORBIS, p. 30; Minnesota Historical Society, p. 31; © Joseph Sohm; ChromoSohm Inc./CORBIS, p. 34; © Patti McConville/Photo Network, p. 40; © Peter Turnley/CORBIS, p. 44; © Markowitz/CORBIS SYGMA, p. 45. Illustrations on p. 48 by Bill Hauser.

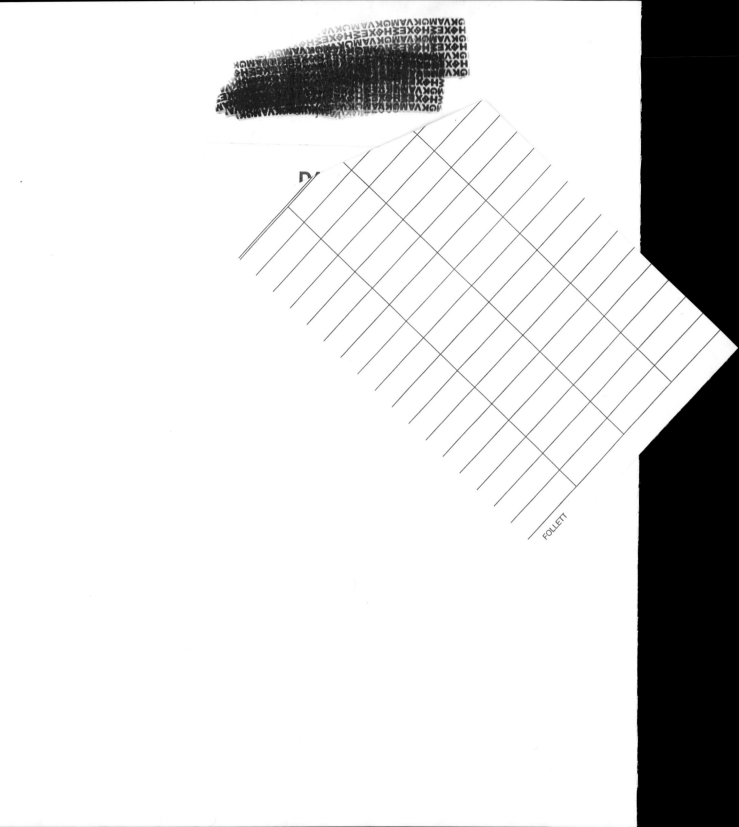